Privatisation, Competition and Regulation

iea

Stephen C. Littlechild

Honorary Professor,
University of Birmingham School of Business

Twenty-ninth Wincott Memorial Lecture at Bishop Partridge Hall, Church House, Westminster, on Thursday, 14 October 1999

The Trustees of the IEA have agreed that any surplus over costs arising from the sale of this Paper should be donated to the Wincott Foundation.

Published by The Institute of Economic Affairs for The Wincott Foundation, 2000

First published in February 2000 by
The Institute of Economic Affairs
2 Lord North Street
Westminster
London SW1P 3LB

© The Wincott Foundation 2000

Occasional Paper 110
ISBN 0073-909X
ISBN 0 255 36480-6

Printed in Great Britain by
Hartington Fine Arts Limited, Lancing,
West Sussex
Set in Times Roman 11 on 13 point

Contents

3

Foreword
Sir Geoffrey Owen

THE PRIVATISATION OF PUBLIC UTILITIES was one of the outstanding achievements of the Conservative governments led by Margaret Thatcher during the 1980s and early 1990s. To conceive and implement this policy required not only political courage of a high order, but also a willingness to examine from first principles how industries which had long been regarded as natural monopolies could be exposed to competition, with consequent gains in lower costs and better service to the consumer. The outcome has been far more successful than even the most enthusiastic advocates of privatisation had hoped. Indeed, this is an area in which Britain can reasonably claim to have set an example to the rest of the world. Other European nations, notably France and Germany, have followed Britain along the same path, as have a growing number of developing countries. Privatisation knowhow has become a major British export.

The impact of these changes in electricity has been particularly impressive. Since privatisation employment has fallen by about one third in electricity transmission and one half in distribution; operating costs have come down by nearly 40 per cent. As the industry became more efficient, prices were reduced sharply. From 1990 to 1999 the price of electricity to business has been reduced in real terms by between 25 per cent and 34 per cent, to domestic consumers by about 26 per cent. At the same time the structure of the industry has been transformed. The two largest generating companies at the time of privatisation, National Power and PowerGen, have seen their share of production come down to well below 30 per cent. Changes in ownership have brought new management and new capital into the industry.

Professor Stephen Littlechild has had a profound influence both on the thinking that led up to privatisation and – as director of the Office of Electricity Regulation from 1989 to 1998 – on the practical implementation of the policy. The Trustees of the Wincott Foundation were therefore delighted when he accepted their invitation to deliver the 1999 Wincott lecture. He provided his listeners with a masterly account of the privatisation process, drawing on lessons from 'Austrian' economists such as Hayek, Mises and Schumpeter as well as exploring the mechanics of the regulatory system. As he stressed in the lecture, one of the innovative features of the British approach to regulation, as opposed to the longer-established American approach, was the focus on price rather than profit. The RPI–X formula gives companies a greater incentive to reduce their costs than US-style rate-of-return regulation, and ensures that the consumers get the benefit of efficiency improvement.

Another distinctive feature of the British system is that it places competition at the forefront, whereas traditional US regulation for the most part suppressed it. Although, as Professor Littlechild says in his lecture, there are still further improvements to be made, a great deal of progress has been made towards the long-term goal of turning what had been a public-sector monopoly into a private, competitive and unregulated industry.

Harold Wincott, the financial journalist in whose honour the Wincott Foundation was set up, was a consistent advocate of competition as the primary regulator of economic activity. Professor Littlechild's lecture was entirely in line with this philosophy, and the published version of the lecture deserves the widest possible readership. As in all IEA publications, the views expressed are those of the author, not of the Institute (which has no corporate views), its Trustees, Advisers or Directors.

December 1999 GEOFFREY OWEN
Chairman of Trustees,
The Wincott Foundation

The Author

PROFESSOR STEPHEN C. LITTLECHILD WAS DIRECTOR GENERAL OF ELECTRICITY SUPPLY (DGES), in charge of the Office of Electricity Regulation (OFFER), from its foundation in September 1989 to December 1998. Previously he advised ministers on the regulatory regime for British Telecom and the water industry. In 1983 he proposed the RPI–X approach to price controls, which has since been widely adopted for regulating utilities in the UK and overseas. He was a member of the Monopolies and Mergers Commission for six years. Before 1989 he acted as a consultant to various public and private sector organisations.

Professor Littlechild graduated as Bachelor of Commerce from the University of Birmingham in 1964. He did post-graduate work at Stanford University 1965/67; Northwestern University 1967/68; the University of Texas at Austin 1968/69, obtaining his PhD there in 1969; and post-doctoral research at UCLA and Northwestern. From 1972 to 1975 he was Professor of Applied Economics at Aston Management Centre. He was Professor of Commerce and Head of the Department of Industrial Economics and Business Studies at the University of Birmingham from 1975 to 1989. During 1979/80 he was a visiting professor or research fellow at Stanford University, New York University, University of Chicago and Virginia Polytechnic and Institute. Since 1994 he has been an Honorary Professor in the University of Birmingham Business School.

Professor Littlechild's publications include *Operational Research for Managers* (Philip Allan, 1976), *The Fallacy of the Mixed Economy* (IEA, 1978), *Elements of Telecommunications Economics* (Institute of Electrical Engineers, 1979), *Energy Strategies for the UK (with K G Vaidya)* (Allen and Unwin, 1982), *Regulation of British Telecommunications' Profitability* (Department of Industry, 1983), *Economic Regulation of Privatised Water Authorities* (HMSO, 1986), and over 60 articles.

Since stepping down as DGES at the end of 1998, Professor Littlechild has engaged in lecturing and consulting for government departments, regulatory bodies, universities, research institutes, regulated companies and international organisations including the World Bank. In May 1999 Stanford University conferred on him the Zale Award for Scholarship and Public Service.

Privatisation, Competition and Regulation
Stephen C. Littlechild

1. Introduction

I AM HONOURED TO BE INVITED TO GIVE THE 29TH WINCOTT LECTURE. Since I used to read the *Investor's Chronicle* in the early 1960s I must have read some of Harold Wincott's work without realising its significance. My excuse for not reading more – and I think it's not a bad one – is that during the early 1960s I was spending more time reading the *City Press*. That publication was surely at least as firm a defender of what Wincott called 'liberal capitalism'. Moreover, it introduced me to the work of two of the many distinguished Wincott lecturers, namely Hayek and Friedman. I want to look at their thinking, among that of others, on the topic of tonight's lecture.

Let me first outline what I am going to say. I begin by asking – why am I here? Or to paraphrase what some of my American friends kept asking me over the last ten years: what's a nice free-market boy like you doing in a place like a regulator's office? This involves first looking at what leading market economists have had to say about public utility regulation. Second, I naturally hope to show that such regulation is a respectable activity for a market economist, at least regulation UK style.

Third, I want to look at what privatisation, competition and regulation have actually achieved in the British electricity industry over the past ten years. I think the record justifies the faith of those who have advocated such policies. Many of these advocates must have given or attended the Wincott lecture series over the past thirty years.

Finally, I want to look forward to some potential developments in utility regulation. Some of these give me hope but others give me cause for concern. I shall make a few suggestions for reform.

2. Views of Austrian Economists on Public Utility Regulation

Since it has been mainly Austrian economist friends questioning my recent choice of career, I begin by looking at what leading Austrian economists have had to say about public utility regulation. This was an agreeable trip down Memory Lane, since Hayek's *Road to Serfdom* was one of the very first books I bought when I went to Birmingham University nearly 40 years ago. Then, during one summer vacation, I devoted an hour each morning to working through each of four learned treatises, two of which were Hayek's *Constitution of Liberty* and Mises' *Human Action*.

Let us start with Schumpeter, whose views on monopoly are always interesting. His argument is as follows:

'...pure cases of long-term monopoly must be of the rarest occurrence...[and] can hardly persist for a period long enough to matter for analysis of total output, unless buttressed by public authority...Even railroads and power and light concerns had first to create the demand for their services and, when they had done so, to defend their market against competition. Outside the field of public utilities, the position of a single seller can in general be conquered – and retained for decades – only on the condition that he does not behave like a monopolist'.[1]

Outside the field of public utilities, this sounds fine provided one has sufficient faith in Schumpeter's perennial gale of creative destruction. But what about *inside* the field of public utilities, where by implication a monopolist *can* behave like a monopolist for decades? Schumpeter seems to have nothing more to say on this.

Now for Mises, writing in the first instance on Socialism. He presents a relatively conventional analysis of monopoly: it leads to a higher market price, greater profit and smaller quantity produced

---

[1] Joseph A Schumpeter, *Capitalism, Socialism and Democracy*, New York, Harper and Row, 1942, 1947 3rd edn. 1950 p.99.

and consumed than under free competition. He notes also that against the smaller production of the monopolised goods must be set the increased production of other goods, but these are less important goods from the customer's perspective. He too takes the view that monopolies are relatively rare, except where protected by state, or

'where the capital required to erect a competing enterprise was not able to count on an adequate return. A railway company can achieve a monopoly where it would not pay to build a competing line, the traffic being too small for two lines to be profitable.'[2]

Mises continues:

'the effect of such monopolies e.g. the railway company or the electric power plant…may be a change in the distribution of income and property which is felt to be disagreeable – at least, by those directly affected.'

I daresay that if Mrs Mises paid the housekeeping bills she may have found it more disagreeable than he did. But should anything be done about such disagreeable situations? Mises says merely that 'the consequences of monopoly must be judged by other standards than the mere catchwords Price Dictation and the Rule of the Trust Magnates' (p.392). But he does not tell us what these other standards are or should be.

A few years later we get Mises' more explicit views in *Human Action*. Utilities now appear as examples of what he calls 'limited space monopoly': the outcome of the fact that physical conditions restrict the field of operation in such a way that only one or a few enterprises can enter it:

_____

2 Ludwig Von Mises, *Socialism: An Economic and Sociological Analysis*, London: Jonathan Cape, 1936, 1951, reprinted 1972. p.391.

11

'There were instances in which two or even more companies shared in supplying the residents of an area with gas, electricity, and telephone service. But even in such exceptional cases there is hardly any real competition. Conditions suggest to the rivals that they combine at least tacitly'.[3]

Is the solution government ownership? Apparently not, since Mises refers briefly (p.856) to the problems of nationalized and municipalized enterprises, which very often result in financial failure, with losses burdening the state or city treasury. Mises points out that this policy depends on the existence of other taxable incomes, and can no longer be resorted to once these other incomes have disappeared.

What about imposing maximum prices in such situations? Mises emphasises that in general this makes things worse from the point of view of those supporting intervention, since it creates shortages of supply. But he admits that this is not necessarily so in the case of monopoly prices:

'The difference between the monopoly price and the competitive price of the commodity in question provides a margin in which maximum prices could be enforced without defeating the ends sought by the government.... The maximum price could re-establish the competitive price and increase demand, production, and the supply offered for sale.'

He says it would be paradoxical to introduce such measures where monopoly prices are the outcome of government interference. However,

'Things are different in those rare instances in which monopoly prices come into existence without assistance from the government. Here governmental maximum prices could re-establish competitive conditions if it were possible to find out by academic computation at which height a non-existing competitive market would have determined the price.'

---

[3] Ludwig Von Mises, *Human Action*, Yale University Press, 1949, 1963 p.375.

This may sound promising, but not so:

> 'That all endeavours to construct non market prices are vain
> has been shown. The unsatisfactory results of all attempts to
> determine what the fair or correct price for the services of
> public utilities should be are well known to all experts.'
> (pp. 766–7)

Mises then goes on to explain why government interference with market prices caused the decline of ancient civilisation, especially the Roman Empire.

I hope that my spell as a regulator has not contributed to the decline of modern civilisation. It seems to me there is a way out here: what if regulation does not attempt the ambitious task of calculating the competitive price, but the more manageable one of limiting the exploitation of the monopoly?

Many commentators, both economists and non-economists, have asserted that the purpose of utility regulation, and of price caps in particular, is to mimic the operation of the competitive market. I myself have never claimed that.[4] I agree with Mises about the difficulty of predicting what a competitive market price could be, particularly in markets characterised by heavy capital investments that are location-specific and have long asset lives. One reason for regulation is precisely because such markets do not operate in the same way as the more familiar commodity markets do. So what if the aim is to calculate and set not a competitive price, but rather a maximum price that is somewhere between the monopoly and competitive levels? In Mises' words, this would need to be 'applied with very great caution within a narrow margin' (p.767), in order to 'safeguard the smooth functioning of social co-operation' (p.722). Mises gives us no reason to suppose that such a device applied to the utility sector will not work, other than the assertion that such incursions into interventionism and the 'social market economy' will ultimately lead to socialism.

---

[4] Nor, I think, did the late Michael Beesley, with whom I developed the RPI–X price cap discussed below, and to whose work, support and influence I paid tribute at the time of delivering this lecture.

Finally, on to Hayek.[5] He begins with a major concern about monopoly:

> 'Apart from the intellectual influences...the impetus of the movement of totalitarianism comes mainly from the two great vested interest groups, organised capital and organised labour....
>
> This movement is, of course, deliberately planned mainly by the capitalist organisers of monopolies.'

This may no longer be as widespread a concern as it was in 1944, when Hayek published *The Road to Serfdom*. Nevertheless I will quote at length because his views are particularly apposite to today's topic.

Where monopoly is inevitable, Hayek seriously doubts whether the best way of controlling it is to put it in the hands of the state, especially if more than one industry is involved:

> 'Even if railways, road and air transport, or the supply of gas and electricity, were all inevitably monopolies, the consumer is unquestionably in a much stronger position so long as they remain separate monopolies than when they are 'co-ordinated' by a central control. Private monopoly is scarcely ever complete and even more rarely of long duration or able to disregard potential competition. But a state monopoly is always a state-protected monopoly – protected against both potential competition and effective criticism. It means in most instances that a temporary monopoly is given the power to secure its position for all time – a power almost certain to be used. Where the power which ought to check and control monopoly becomes interested in sheltering and defending its appointees, where for the government to remedy an abuse is to admit responsibility for it and where criticism of the actions

---

[5] F. A. Hayek, *The Road to Serfdom*, London: Routledge and Kegan Paul, 1944, pp. 146–7.

of monopoly mean criticism of the government, there is little hope of monopoly becoming the servant of the community.'

What is the preferable alternative?

'The probability is that wherever monopoly is really inevitable the plan which used to be preferred by the Americans, of a strong state control over private monopolies, if consistently pursued, offers a better chance of satisfactory results than state management. This would at least seem to be so where the state enforces a stringent price control which leaves no room for extraordinary profits in which others than the monopolists can participate. Even if this should have the effect (as it sometimes had with American public utilities) that the services of the monopolistic industries would become less satisfactory than they might be, this would be a small price to pay for an effective check on the powers of monopoly. Personally I should much prefer to have to put up with some such inefficiency than have organised monopoly control my ways of life.'

After this brief survey, what are we to make of the Austrian view of utility regulation? There seems to be a general consensus that monopoly is not as widespread or permanent or problematic as generally believed; that such monopoly as does exist is most likely attributable to government restrictions; that regulation of potentially competitive markets is likely to induce shortages or be counter-productive; and that a little intervention is likely to breed more. It is difficult to disagree with most of this. But utilities are acknowledged as an exceptional case, where the previous arguments about monopoly and against regulation do not necessarily apply. Government ownership of utilities is considered to be undesirable because it is likely to be loss-making or too powerful, and likely to prolong the monopoly. Contrary to the implied views of my Austrian friends, I find no argument by Mises against utility regulation (indeed he tacitly accepts the possibility

15

of intervention to facilitate social co-operation) and there is positive support for utility regulation from Hayek.[6]

3. Friedman on Utility Regulation

Hayek's analysis is the closest we get among the Austrians of an appraisal of the case for and against regulation in the light of the characteristics of regulated and unregulated utilities. To find a more explicit albeit still concise assessment we may turn to Milton Friedman, who gave the first Wincott lecture, although not on this topic:

'...when technical conditions make monopoly the natural outcome of competitive market forces, there are only three alternatives that seem available: private monopoly, public monopoly, or public regulation [of private monopoly].

All three are bad so we must choose among evils... I reluctantly conclude that, if tolerable, private monopoly may be the least of the evils.'[7]

His justification is as follows:

---

[6] Other Austrian economists have written on the topic. Murray Rothbard, not entirely surprisingly, seems to take Mises' argument to a further extreme. He notes that 'limited space monopoly' is just one case in which only one firm in a field is profitable. But he argues that '..."monopoly" is a meaningless appellation, unless monopoly price is achieved, and there is no way of determining whether the price charged for the good is a "monopoly price" or not ... [So] All prices on the free market are competitive.... Thus we conclude that there is "nothing wrong" with "monopoly price". Murray N. Rothbard, *Man, Economy and State*, Los Angeles, Nash Publishing, 1962, 1970 (pp.614, 619) I hope I am not alone in finding Rothbard's argument unpersuasive. Israel Kirzner has argued that 'intervention [in the form of government regulation] tends to interfere harmfully in the *entrepreneurial process* upon which the most basic of the market's virtues ... must surely depend.' Israel M Kirzner, *The Perils of Regulation: A Market-Process Approach*, Coral Gables: University of Miami School of Law, Law and Economics Center, 1978, p. 2. I refer later to Kirzner's argument.

[7] Milton Friedman, *Capitalism and Freedom*, Chicago, University of Chicago Press, 1962 p.28.

'If society were static so that the conditions which give rise to a technical monopoly were sure to remain, I would have little confidence in this solution. In a rapidly changing society, however, the conditions making for technical monopoly frequently change and I suspect that both public regulation and public monopoly are likely to be less responsive to such changes in conditions, to be less readily capable of elimination, than private monopoly'.

After giving the example of railroad regulation, which he suggests has prevented the emergence of a competitive market, he continues:

'The choice between the evils of private monopoly, public monopoly, and public regulation cannot, however, be made once and for all, independently of the factual circumstances. If the technical monopoly is of a service or commodity that is regarded as essential and if its monopoly power is sizeable, even the short run effects of private unregulated monopoly may not be tolerable, and either public regulation or ownership may be a lesser evil'. (p.29)

He concludes with the remark that:

'Technical monopoly may on occasion justify a *de facto* public monopoly. It cannot by itself justify a public monopoly achieved by making it illegal for anyone else to compete'.

In a later publication he indicates that a public monopoly is much worse than a private monopoly (regulated or unregulated) because it tends to be more inefficient.

4. The Arguments for Utility Regulation

Hayek and Friedman thus share many concerns but come to a different conclusion. I am sympathetic to Friedman's reasoning, and I am not sure that I would argue against him as applied to most regulated monopolies in the USA during the period in which he was writing. But I want to argue now for a conclusion closer to that of Hayek, in the case of the UK and most other countries over the last decade or so, and for at least some time into the future.

I have three main arguments to make.

The *first* is that the alternative of an unregulated private monopoly is typically not politically available in the context of privatising those public monopolies such as the utilities, where the service is indeed regarded as essential and the monopoly power is indeed sizeable.

The *second* argument is that, in areas where competition is not deemed feasible, incentive regulation seeks to promote the kind of efficiency improvements that might be more associated with competitive industries than with regulated monopolies.

Third, what I might call UK style utility regulation has challenged the notion that these industries have to be monopolies: it has explicitly encouraged new entry and promoted competition where it seems possible to do so, thereby seeking to minimise the disadvantage identified by both Hayek and Friedman with regulated monopoly.

In consequence, I would argue that the relevant choice for almost all countries today is whether to convert a public utility monopoly into a privately owned but regulated industry, and the real question is how this can best be done so as to maximise the scope for competition. The longer-term aim is to turn as much as possible of that industry into a private, competitive and unregulated industry rather than a private monopoly. In the short term this may necessitate a considerable role for regulation. There may however be further steps that can be taken to reduce the adverse impact of regulation. Let me now expand on these arguments.

Political Constraints

British Telecommunications (BT) was the first British utility to be considered for privatisation, in the early 1980s. The only way that the transition from public to private ownership could be made acceptable was by pointing to the US experience to demonstrate that private ownership provided superior efficiency and service, and that protection to customers was afforded by regulation. The form of that regulation in Britain was for discussion, but the principle of it was not.

This attitude held throughout all the British utility privatisations, and it is difficult to quarrel with it. Subsequent experience suggests that, for the first decade at least, and in many respects for much longer, the incumbent companies in each of the privatised utilities could and would have continued to increase prices in the absence of regulation. In contrast, regulation (plus private ownership and competition) has for the most part led to real price reductions.

Some economists might argue that what counts is the sum of benefits to producers and consumers, not the benefits to customers alone. Distribution is not a matter for them. But that is not the political world we live in. Although there is now a general acceptance (in Britain, but not yet in many developing countries) that utility revenue must cover costs, including a sufficient return on capital, this is certainly not to say that price does not matter. And understandably so. At one end of the customer spectrum are the so-called 'fuel poor', whose fuel consumption takes such a high proportion of their incomes that every additional pound spent on fuel is a pound less for food, clothing or housing. At the other end of the spectrum are the industrial users for whom international competitiveness is crucial, and on whose success depend the jobs and income of millions of families. If regulation can reduce prices below monopoly levels and down towards cost (however defined), without compromising new entry, competition, choice, innovation, and other longer-term attributes of a competitive market, then there is understandable pressure for it. In such circumstances, appropriate regulation can provide 'the smooth functioning of social co-operation', at least during the transition to a competitive market.

To the best of my knowledge, almost all countries that have privatised their utilities over the last decade have taken the same view and accompanied privatisation by regulation, except the Czech Republic, Russia and New Zealand. The Czech Republic and Russia were both so concerned to secure the transfer to private ownership, and to reduce the role of government, that they decided against regulation, and are now having to deal with the resulting problems of monopoly. I am not familiar with the situations in detail, and they differ between the two countries, but I have the impression that there are difficult problems yet to resolve.

New Zealand's experience is perhaps the most instructive for developed countries. That country had such a bad experience of price regulation during the 1950s and 1960s that it resolved not to reintroduce it. (It is also relevant that the initial stages of reform in New Zealand were limited to corporatisation and the introduction of competition, without private ownership.) But the morning I arrived there in April 1999, I heard the electricity companies announcing price increases. The media took pleasure in showing recent footage of the minister looking forward to substantial price reductions in the near future. Civil servants told me at lunchtime that they would be recommending price control. That evening the deputy minister said that he would of course be looking at the possibility of price regulation. A couple of months later the Government introduced a bill to provide for price regulation of the electricity industry.

Advantages of Incentive Regulation

My second argument is that the principal method we have developed to regulate UK utilities has been an improvement over the traditional method of regulating US utilities, on which both Hayek's and Friedman's evaluation would have been based. As is now well known, we have focused on price rather than profit. The RPI–X price cap allows prices to increase (or requires prices to reduce) at X per cent below the Retail Price Index, which is a measure of inflation, for a specified number of years. This gives assurance to investors, managers and customers. It also gives greater efficiency incentives to companies in the short term. Customers benefit from the prospect of the resulting increased efficiency being passed to them over time, when the price cap is reset.[8] Where

---

[8] Israel Kirzner has argued that even if one imagines a regulatory official dedicated to ensuring the adoption of all known possible measures for cutting costs, 'one can hardly imagine him discovering, except by the sheerest accident, those opportunities for increasing efficiency of which he is completely unaware. The official is not subject to the entrepreneurial profit incentive.... Nothing within the regulatory process seems able to simulate, even remotely well, the discovery process that is so integral to the unregulated market.' (*The Perils of Regulation* p.16) The strength of the RPI–X approach is that it harnesses the incentives of the management within the market context, and does not require the official to know or discover the opportunities in question.

necessary, prescribed minimum standards can ensure that cost and price reductions are not at the expense of quality of service.

This development changed the view of at least one influential minister about the desirability of utility privatisation. Nicholas Ridley had been asked to plan the Conservative privatisation policy for 1979. He had not recommended privatising natural monopolies because he was convinced at that time by the argument that there would be no gain from putting a monopoly into private hands. However, he changed his mind:

> 'the argument that price control would leave no scope for incentives to improve collapsed when the American system of price control was rejected...The problem was solved by the introduction of Professor Littlechild's formula RPI–X'.[9]

UK Regulation Promotes Competition

My third argument is that UK privatisation and regulation have increasingly put competition at the forefront, whereas traditional US regulation for the most part suppressed it. Traditional texts on US regulation, including economic ones, for the most part ignored it.[10]

The emphasis on competition goes back to before the privatisation of BT. The government had set up Mercury as a competitor to BT. Michael Beesley had urged more competition in his report on resale of lines. The Act privatising BT instructed the

---

[9] Nicholas Ridley, '*My Style of Government*' The Thatcher Years, Hutchinson 1991, p 62. For other ministerial views acknowledging the role of RPI–X, see Margaret Thatcher, *The Downing Street Years*, London: Harper Collins, ch. 23; Nigel Lawson, *The View from No. 11*, London: Bantam Press, 1993, chs. 18–20; and Kenneth Baker, *The Turbulent Years*, London: Faber and Faber, 1993, ch. 4.

[10] In 1969 one authoritative text on US public utilities devoted just $2\frac{1}{2}$ of its 774 pages to the then-novel concept of strengthening the forces of market competition. For further discussion, see M. E. Beesley and S. C. Littlechild, 'The regulation of privatized monopolies in the United Kingdom', *RAND Journal of Economics*, Vol. 20, No. 3, Autumn 1989, pp. 454–72, esp. pp. 464–8. The text in question, which was inadvertently omitted from the list of references in the article, was Charles F. Phillips, Jr., *The Economics of Regulation*, Homewood, Illinois: Richard D. Irwin, 1965, revised ed. 1969.

regulator and the Secretary of State to maintain and promote effective competition in telecommunications. When I was asked to advise on regulating BT's profitability, I emphasised that the problem only arose because of the absence of competition. I pointed out that competition could be allowed and encouraged in a number of ways – for example, by removing BT's monopoly of the 'first instrument'. RPI–X would only be a means of 'holding the fort' until competition arrived.[11] In the event the government did not feel able to allow as much competition in telecommunications as quickly as some of us would have liked. But there undoubtedly has been increasing competition and new entry and innovation in the British telecommunications industry, and the previous telecom regulator claimed that the price control he set would be the last. (It certainly was *his* last.)

The extent of competition initially provided in the privatised utilities has varied, and again has been less than many commentators would have liked. But it has increased with successive privatisations, and has generally been more than the industry and the merchant banks would have preferred. In all the utility sectors, the regulators have been required to promote competition and have done so. Let me give two early examples from electricity, which may seem trivial but incredible now, but were very real at the time.

A new entrant into generation requires a licence. It would have been possible for me as regulator to have assessed the need for further investment, the best location and fuel type, and the most suitable applicant, no doubt hearing from the incumbent companies why further investment by others was not necessary, and then granted or not granted a licence for each new plant accordingly. This was broadly the policy in airline regulation. At least one informed and influential commentator is still making that argument nowadays, with the added recommendation that the chosen plant and site could then be put up for auction. I decided against this approach. It was for generators themselves to take

[11] Stephen C Littlechild, *Regulation of British Telecommunications' Profitability*, London: Department of Industry, February 1983. For a ministerial view on this process, see Baker, op.cit.

their own views on these matters, and to back their judgements with investment. Moreover, it would be undesirable to raise obstacles against new entrants that were non-existent against incumbents. In practice, I ensured that all new applicants for generation licences got them, and all licences gave the same unlimited access to the whole of the country for any type of plant, as did the licences of the incumbents.

Competition in supply was initially more tricky. It was an entirely novel concept. (We did not know at that time that it existed in rudimentary form in Chile, and it would not have helped politically if we had). I felt strongly that competition in generation would not be fully effective if the purchasers from those generators had a monopoly over sales to final customers, not least because it was difficult to prevent some pass-through of generation costs incurred by suppliers. Nor would customers themselves be effectively protected. But how to provide for competition to final customers without the uneconomic provision of multiple wires in each street? The inspiration came from the precedent of telecommunications, and from the use of system arrangements envisaged for electricity transmission. The key was to let generators and other suppliers have the right of access to the distribution systems in each area.

At first the idea met with profound scepticism. A senior civil servant in the Department of Energy, responsible for the privatisation programme, told me that only a customer as large as ICI (accounting for about one per cent of national consumption) would want to buy directly from a generator. And neither generators nor distribution companies (the former Area Boards as suppliers) would want to bother with seeking out individual small customers. I persevered, but the extent of acceptance of this concept at that time can be judged from the small reference that I managed to get into the White Paper. Whereas competition in generation gets several pages, mainly on how the generators will have to compete to supply the national grid or the distribution companies, competition in supply gets three ultra-cautious sentences:

'The distribution companies themselves will also have to bid for part of their business in a competitive environment. Adjacent distribution companies could find themselves competing to supply large users near their common borders. And large users will also be able to buy electricity direct from generators, by-passing the distribution companies but using their transmission and distribution systems for 'common carriage' of the electricity.'[12]

The next thing that worried me, now as prospective regulator, was the draft wording in the Electricity Bill. Section 6(2) said, and still says, that the Secretary of State and the Director 'may grant a licence authorising any person to supply electricity to any premises specified or of a description specified in the licence'. The initial second-tier licence granted by the government to National Power on 26 March 1990 (just before Vesting) contained two and half pages of names and addresses of its industrial customers. It was clearly intended that a supplier had to argue for its licence to be extended every time it wanted to sign a new customer. Moreover, when it made such an application it had to publish a copy of the application within fourteen days, and when the Director made such a licence extension he was required to notify the public electricity suppliers in whose areas these disloyal customers were located. How on earth could competition in supply become effective if competitors were faced with such obstacles? And how could Offer cope with such a bureaucratic workload if, as I hoped, customers would be changing supplier all the time?

I explained to Willie Rickett, the departmental official co-ordinating the privatisation process, that I would want to consider the possibility of writing the licence so as to enable a licensee to supply all customers in the competitive market, thereby avoiding this process. I asked if the wording of the Bill could be changed to make sure that this was possible. He was adamant that all concerned would be aghast at such a radical proposition, and anyway there was no way the idea could be introduced at such a late stage. But he promised to do what he could. The result was

---

[12] *Privatising Electricity*, London, HMSO, Cm 322, February 1988, p. 11.

a sentence slipped into the otherwise obscure section 111, entitled 'General interpretation'. The first few clauses simply explain that 'the Director' means the Director General of Electricity Supply, and so on. Then comes a remarkable sentence. 'For the purposes of this Act any class or description may be framed by reference to any matters or circumstances whatever.' This gave me the assurance I needed, 'for the avoidance of doubt', as the lawyers say. When Scottish Hydro Electric applied to me for a second-tier licence it did so with a list of customers following the precedent set for National Power. I granted this licence on 28 June 1990, so that the company could begin to compete in the market. But I also enquired whether the company would find it more convenient to have a licence couched in more general terms. It indicated that it would, and on 6 July 1990 I granted an extension to the whole of the above 1 MW market. All second-tier licences have been in that form ever since.

5. Competition and Regulation in the British Electricity Industry.

So far I have argued that British privatisation policy, and the associated regulatory framework, have been oriented to securing efficiency by the use of price controls rather than profit controls and have explicitly required the promotion of competition. But has this policy been effective? I turn now to a brief summary of the experience in the electricity industry.

Competition in Generation

After the government had privatised BT and British Gas intact, there were criticisms that it was simply transferring ownership of monopolies. Cecil Parkinson, Secretary of State for Energy, decided to restructure electricity by separating off transmission and breaking up the generation sector, eventually into three companies. Nonetheless, critics referred to the 'duopoly' of National Power and PowerGen, which together accounted for nearly 80 per cent of the market in England and Wales at the beginning, and noted that Nuclear Electric accounted for almost all the rest of the market.

Since then, a combination of market incentives and regulatory policy has enabled competition to develop.

First, the interconnectors immediately increased their market share by increasing throughput to fill existing capacity and soon took steps to extend the capacity of the Scottish interconnector.

Second, the nuclear stations, considered too expensive and risky to privatise initially, have increased output by about 75 per cent, mostly from more efficient management. Two-thirds of those stations have now been privatised.

Third, new entrants brought new technology such as combined cycle gas turbines other new ideas to the industry, and accounted for 17 per cent of the generation market by 1998/99.[13]

Fourth, National Power and PowerGen agreed to divest a total of 6 GW of existing coal-fired plant, which was purchased by Eastern Electricity and subsequently run at higher output than it previously had been.

The structure of the generation market has thus significantly changed over time, as shown in Table 1.

Nine years on, the duopoly was only half the size it was at Vesting. In 1998/99 National Power and PowerGen accounted for under 40 per cent of the generation market. Their share has since reduced even further, as described below. They are no longer a duopoly. Over 60 generation licensees supply the remaining output with further projects under construction and more seeking to enter the market.

Competitive pressures on gas prices and equipment installation costs, improvements in fuel efficiency, and innovative contractual risk sharing arrangements have brought down the new entry price. There is also evidence of efficiency improvements that would not have happened anyway as a result of external factors, including the significantly increased output from existing capacity. In addition, staffing levels at the largest generating companies have fallen by about two-thirds. Part of this reduction reflects plant disposals to Eastern and the use of newer technology but much reflects increased productivity from existing plant. Moreover, the

---

[13] This proportion had increased to over 20 per cent by the year ending October 1999.

Table 1: Generation market shares (%) England and Wales

	1989/90*	1990/91	1994/95	1998/99
National Power	48	45·5	34	21
PowerGen	30	28·5	26	18
Eastern	0	0	1	9.5
Nuclear Electric	16	17·5	22	17
Magnox Electric	0	0	0	8
Scottish interconnector	1·5	1·5	3	3
French interconnector	3·5	6	6	4·5
Pumped storage	0·5	0·5	0·5	1
Others	0·5	0·5	1	1
New entrants	0	0	6·5	17
Total (%)	100	100	100	100
Total Output (TWh)	256	267	274	295

*Hypothetical attribution based on allocation of plant at privatisation.

Source: Offer Reports

incentives and ability to secure such improvements, to negotiate lower fuel prices and more flexible contracts and to introduce new technology would not have existed to anything like the same degree without the pressures of private ownership and competition.

Despite these steps, competition in generation is not yet fully effective. In 1998 System Marginal Price (SMP) in the Pool, which is the price received by all generators, was still set more than two-thirds of the time by the largest two generators, and almost all the time by only four generators. There is still scope to exercise substantial market power. Pool prices are still some 10–20 per cent above the present new entry level based on the latest gas-fired plant. Following regulatory pressure the two largest companies are both in course of divesting more plant as part of their merger and acquisition strategies. This will reduce their aggregate market share from about 40 per cent in 1998/99 to around 25 per cent. It is not so clear how far it will increase the number of generators setting Pool price.

The position on generation competition has been exacerbated by the present government's decision to adopt a policy of stricter consents on the building of new gas-fired power stations. The previous government had not used such consents to restrict new entry. The present government's view is that distortions in the electricity market, including in the Pool, have disadvantaged coal, and that these distortions need to be put right before further gas consents can routinely be given. On this basis a large number of potential entrants wishing to build gas-fired plant have been frustrated. I have elsewhere expressed my view that the stricter consents policy is now the major obstacle to a more competitive electricity market.[14] I return to this later.

Competition to Supply Industrial Customers

In contrast to the fears of sceptics, customers and competitive suppliers have warmly welcomed competition. The largest 5,000 or so customers, with maximum demand above 1 MW, were allowed to choose their own supplier immediately on privatization in 1990. They accounted for about a third of total electricity demand. The next 50,000 or so customers, with a maximum demand of 100 kW to 1 MW, were allowed to choose their supplier in 1994. These customers, who included the supermarkets and fast food chains, brought the proportion of the total market open to competition up to about half. The remaining 26 million customers, including smaller businesses and domestic, were scheduled to have access to competition in 1998.

Immediately the market was open, over 40 per cent of the large customer market was competed away to new suppliers, principally the large generators. The extent of second-tier supply (that is, supply by firms other than the previous local supplier) has steadily increased over time for all sizes of customer. Now, about 80 per cent of the large customer market (with maximum demand above 1 MW) is supplied second-tier and over 60 per cent of the medium-size (above 100 kW) market (Figure 1).

---

[14] For example, in 'Achievements, challenges and concerns', *Electricity UK*, London: Electricity Association, Number 36, January 1999, pp. 6–9.

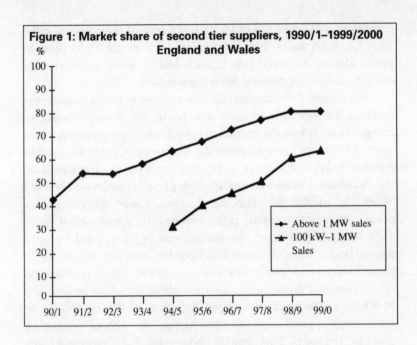

Figure 1: Market share of second tier suppliers, 1990/1–1999/2000 England and Wales

Legend:
- Above 1 MW sales
- 100 kW–1 MW Sales

Competition to Supply Domestic Customers

In the light of this experience, considerable thought was given to the basis of introducing competition to domestic customers. Customer profiles were introduced to avoid the costs of new half-hourly metering. Distribution companies had to modify their IT systems to record the registration and transfer of customers and to facilitate metering, billing and settlement, including the proper application of use of system charges and provision of other services to competitors. These systems needed to be tested and made consistent across 14 companies, the Pool and many suppliers. This was a major logistical exercise, and it fell to the regulator to organize it because no one else had the incentive and ability to do so. It was decided to phase the opening of the small customer market, both within and between regional companies, between September 1998 and June 1999. In fact the market was fully open by the end of May 1999, some weeks ahead of that schedule.

The process was not cheap, and some have asked whether it will be worthwhile for domestic customers, given the costs involved. The cost of the competition arrangements to domestic customers will be of the order of 1 per cent of their annual bills. This has been more than compensated for by the reductions in prices already achieved (see below), and by the price offers and other benefits now flowing from competition.

Transitional price controls have been used to protect customers pending the opening of each tranche of the supply market to competition. When the market for medium-sized customers was opened to competition in 1994, the supply price controls that had previously applied to them were removed. (The price controls on the distribution networks remained in place, as discussed below.) When the market for domestic customers was opened, it was prudent to maintain supply price restraints on a transitional basis. This was partly because the market was being opened up on a phased basis, so not all customers would be able to exercise choice immediately, and partly because the extent, development and effectiveness of domestic competition could not easily be assessed in advance. However, I changed the form of the controls. The initial supply price controls allowed pass-through of generation costs to customers. This seemed undesirable and unnecessary in a competitive market. The new transitional supply price restraints specified fixed maximum prices. This transferred the price risk associated with generation from customers to suppliers, gave clearer protection to customers and provided a stronger incentive on suppliers to purchase and contract efficiently. The additional risk meant leaving a greater margin for suppliers, but customers were protected since they could move to another supplier if better offers could be sustained in the market.

These restraints provided for initial price reductions averaging about 6 per cent in real terms from March 1998, and a further 3 per cent from March 1999. This enabled us to say that all customers would be better off in the new competitive regime. But it was important not to set these restraints so tight as to discourage new entry or stifle the entrepreneurial discovery process. Further price reductions are indeed available in the competitive market. The price reductions offered vary by area, by type of customer and by payment system. For a customer on a standard domestic tariff paying quarterly in arrears, the average level of price reduction is about 4 per cent on a typical annual bill of about £250. The best offers range between 8 and 15 per cent reduction, with a median of about 10 per cent.

What has been the response of customers? By the end of September 1999 some 3.3 million domestic customers, over 12 per cent of the total number, had registered to change supplier, often buying gas as well as electricity from their new supplier. The rate of switching is still about 80,000 customers per week. At this rate some 15 per cent of the domestic market could well have chosen a new supplier by the end of 1999.[15] Experience in the market for larger customers suggests that this proportion will continue to increase over time.

Price Controls on the Transmission and Distribution Networks

RPI–X price controls on the transmission and distribution networks have protected customers. Coupled with stock market pressures, they have also given companies the incentive to reduce costs significantly after some initial variations in the first few years. For example, manpower reductions have been of the order of one-third in transmission and one-half in distribution. (As in generation, these have essentially been achieved voluntarily). Operating costs net of depreciation were reduced by nearly 40 per cent in transmission from the average of the first 3 years (1990/91 to 1992/93) to 1997/98, and by about 27 per cent on average for the 12 regional distribution companies from 1992/3 to 1997/98.

In retrospect the initial price controls and capital structures set by the Government at privatisation underestimated the scope for efficiency savings and increased borrowing by companies. The resulting increases in profits and stock market prices, partly due to newly allowed merger activity, caused widespread public concern. However, the process of revising and tightening the controls has ensured that benefits have increasingly gone to customers. The revised controls put in place in 1995 and 1996 reduced charges for use of the distribution system by between 20 and 30 per cent,

---

[15] At the end of October 1999, nearly 4 million domestic customers had registered to change supplier, about 14·5 per cent of the total, and the rate of switching was running at about 90,000 customers per week.

followed by RPI–3 for the next 4 years. This was equivalent in real terms to reductions in distribution charges of nearly 10 per cent a year, every year for the 5-year duration of the revised controls. This was worth around £4 billion (about $6.4 billion) to users over the period of the controls.

In August and October 1999 the present regulator published draft proposals for revised distribution price controls for the subsequent period.[16] These envisaged further reductions in distribution charges of around 25 per cent in April 2000 (of which on average about 8 per cent were a transfer of costs from the distribution businesses to the supply businesses), followed by RPI–3 for the next 5 years.

Broadly similar comments apply to transmission charges. In 1997 charges were reduced by 20 per cent followed by RPI–4 for 4 years. This was worth about £1 billion (about $1.6 billion) to users. The next transmission price control review will start shortly.

Prices to Customers

Competition, price controls and a reduction in the fossil fuel levy with the privatisation of Nuclear Electric have reduced prices to all groups of customers, ranging from large industrial to domestic. Figure 2 shows that, by the first quarter of 1999, price reductions to different sizes of industrial customers have been in the range 25–34 per cent in real terms, compared to prices at privatization.

Price reductions to domestic customers, calculated from relevant published tariffs, were around 26 per cent in real terms by April 1999. As noted above, further reductions of around 8–15 per cent were available from the opening of competition in domestic supply during 1999.

Customers are concerned not only about price, but also about quality. Standards of Performance have been set for the main measurable aspect of this, and in many cases penalty payments to customers are made if the Standards are not met. Companies' performance against these Standards is published each year. This

---

[16] *Review of Public Electricity Suppliers 1998 to 2000: Distribution Price Control Review, Draft Proposals*, The Office of Gas and Electricity Markets, August 1999. Letter to the Chief Executives of PES Distribution Businesses, 8 October 1999.

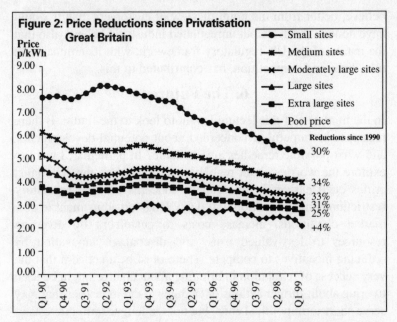

Figure 2: Price Reductions since Privatisation Great Britain

Price p/kWh

Legend:
- Small sites
- Medium sites
- Moderately large sites
- Large sites
- Extra large sites
- Pool price

Reductions since 1990
- 30%
- 34%
- 33%
- 31%
- 25%
- +4%

has proved to be an effective way of improving performance. No company likes to be at the bottom of the league table in any dimension of performance, particularly since this is one way by which stock market analysts and investors can judge management ability. The Standards also facilitate effective management within the companies, and some companies have linked management remuneration to performance against the Standards.

At the time of a price control review, companies submit five-year investment proposals. These are scrutinized carefully and generally challenged, but the price controls have allowed necessary increases in investment. Annual investment in the distribution network has increased by about half since privatization. The average number of interruptions per customer is down and the average number of minutes lost is about half what it was before privatization.

Much more could be said – for example the number of customer complaints about the companies is down by over 60 per cent – but I hope to have given a sufficient flavour of what has been happening. This account shows that the industry under private ownership and subject to competition has performed significantly better than it did as a public sector monopoly and, I believe, better from the point of view of customers than it would have done as a private but unregulated industry. I believe also that the nature of the UK regulatory framework, with its emphasis on incentives and competition, has contributed to this.

6. The Future

In the final part of this lecture I want to look to the future. Is there reason to be hopeful or concerned about potential developments, and what possible remedies are available? In particular, I want to explore the worries about regulation expressed by the economist critics cited earlier. In brief, these concerns are that regulatory restrictions on competition will delay long-run adjustment to new market conditions, increase costs to customers by diverting resources to less-valued uses, and discourage innovation by reducing incentives to compete. There must be a concern that the very success of regulation in bringing about change might be used to bring about further actions or changes in the industries that may serve short-term political ends, but not the longer-term interests of customers. Are there further steps that might be taken to alleviate these worries, and to bring forward the possibility of de-regulating the energy sector?

Let us start with the bill that the government hopes to put before Parliament later this year.[17] It has three main aims:

- To make certain reforms in the regulatory framework
- To merge the Directors General of Electricity Supply and Gas Supply into one office
- To provide for separate licensing of the supply and distribution activities of the public electricity suppliers.

Taking these in reverse order, separate licensing of supply and distribution is much needed. It will enable significant restructuring of the industry to be considered, particularly involving the separate ownership of distribution and supply businesses, without

---

[17] A Utility Regulation Bill was subsequently proposed in the Queen's Speech on 17 November 1999, reflecting the Government's earlier Green Paper *A Fair Deal for Consumers*, DTI, CM 3898, March 1998.

the threat to the ability to regulate each function separately. Each such case will have to be considered on its merits, but done properly such restructuring could increase efficiency, competition and the effectiveness of regulation.

Merging gas and electricity regulation is not without its disadvantages. As noted, Hayek was particularly concerned about 'co-ordination' by a central control. It will concentrate political power and workload, and there is a transitional dislocation to staff. But the commercial and regulatory interactions are increasingly great, and it is understandable that there is pressure to regulate these industries together.

As regards the proposed reform of the regulatory framework, some of the proposals may be helpful (for example, enhancing the regulators' ability to publish more information). Others are unnecessary (for example, requiring the regulators to consult each other and specifying the content of their annual reports). Yet others do not seem supportive of effective and independent regulation (for example, having the government specify how regulators should set price controls). It is important for regulatory processes to be transparent, for decisions to be explained, and for consistency to be achieved wherever appropriate. But if this was not the case initially, there have been significant improvements in regulatory practice subsequently. Only a few days ago the regulators for all the utility industries issued a joint statement explaining that they were formalising and intensifying their joint working relationship. It is not clear that further statutory constraint is either necessary or helpful.

One proposed change here is of greater concern. Utility regulators at present have a primary duty (among others) to promote competition, and a secondary duty (again among others) to protect the interests of customers. (The precise words vary from one Act to another.) The government's Green Paper proposes to replace this by a single primary duty to protect the interests of consumers, wherever possible and appropriate through promoting effective competition.[18] Most regulators felt that making the protection of customers a primary duty was not a problem but

---

[18] *A Fair Deal for Consumers*, p. 15.

largely unnecessary, since they were already required to protect the interests of customers, and sought to do so. But the proposed wording of the change here may be positively unhelpful insofar as it puts an additional obstacle in the way of regulators promoting competition. The duty to promote competition will no longer be unqualified; this will have to be demonstrated to be the most appropriate way to protect customers. The Green Paper notes that in defining the interests of consumers, due weight should be given to their longer- and medium-term interests as well as their immediate or short-term interests. But as Hayek and others have pointed out, the long-run benefits of competition, in terms of innovation and flexibility, are never easy to prove in any particular case. There will be no shortage of companies willing to argue the opposite, perhaps even to the Competition Commission and via judicial review to the Courts.

Are there other reforms that might be considered? Whereas some people are pressing to re-establish a greater role for government, and greater control and influence over the regulators, in my view the interests of customers would be better served by further moves in the opposite direction.

For example, the Government's decision last year to enforce a 'stricter consents' policy on proposals for new electricity generation stations is of concern in several respects. By preventing substantial new entry it precludes the most effective means of reducing the market power of existing generators. The policy is certainly the most significant obstacle to a more competitive market at present. It increases uncertainty in the market. It illustrates the concerns about special pleading to which economists often allude. Political rather than economic considerations are now influencing the type and location of generation. For example, the Government has authorised several smaller combined heat and power plants, but refused consents for small peaking plants that are helpful in reducing market power and in augmenting capacity and security of supply when most needed. It has also refused consent in Scotland, where more competition is most urgently needed, and in the south-west where security and cost of supply are serious issues, but allowed a large gas-fired plant in Wales. One newspaper commented as follows:

'As soon as a better political cause came along – like winning the Welsh Assembly elections – New Labour conveniently forgot about its balanced fuel policy and allowed BP to build a whopper of a station in Baglan Bay.'[19]

The power to issue or refuse consents for each new generation plant maintains an unnecessary and on balance undesirable role for government in the energy sector. Such power is difficult to reconcile with a competitive market, and could usefully be removed. At the very least, the previously unused provisions for consents under the 1976 Energy Act, which are a hangover from a previous and anti-competitive philosophy, should be brought under the umbrella of the Electricity Act, so that their effects on competition and customers have to be taken properly into account.

The job of the regulator is to monitor compliance with licences and, where he or she deems this appropriate, to take steps to modify them. In the energy sector the Secretary of State has an unconstrained power to veto agreed licence modifications proposed by the regulator. He can similarly veto the Director's licence modification references to the Competition Commission. In contrast, in the telecommunications sector these abilities to veto are limited to situations 'where it appears to the Secretary of State to be requisite or expedient to do so in the interests of national security or relations with the government of a country or territory outside the UK'. If a choice has to be made as between regulator and government in these matters, my guess is that constraining the veto power as in the telecommunications wording would make the development of the industry less susceptible to political influence and more likely to promote the interests of customers.

The regulators do not have power to make merger references nor directly to advise the Secretary of State on Commission issues. The government has recently proposed that in the majority of cases the Director General of Fair Trading should take decisions on merger references.[20] The Secretary of State said 'I believe merger

---

[19] Editorial in the *Independent*, 9 September 1999.

[20] *Mergers: A consultation document on proposals for reform*, DTI, October 1999.

cases should be taken out of the political arena. The system would be significantly improved if the vast majority of decisions were taken by independent competition authorities rather than by politicians.'[21] The same argument would apply to energy mergers, and the proposal is a welcome one.

At Vesting, the government took Golden Shares in all the successor electricity companies. It used these shares to discourage mergers and take-overs. After five years the Regional Electricity Company (REC) Golden Shares expired, and there was a burst of merger activity. This reflected active (and hitherto pent-up) competition in the capital market, and has facilitated restructuring and new management. Government already has power to prevent mergers and take-overs if the Commission finds them against the public interest, or to impose conditions for allowing them to proceed, and it has used this power on several occasions. It is not clear what justification remains for continuing to hold Golden Shares in the larger generators, NGC and the two Scottish companies.

Finally, what of the conduct of regulation itself? I fear I cannot escape this topic entirely, so let me restrict myself to a few brief comments on recent and prospective electricity regulation.

I welcome the fact that the proposals on the distribution price control review are broadly consistent with the procedures we set up in the previous review. Naturally there are differences of detail but the underlying principles and calculations remain consistent. I do not comment on the numbers but I guess that the Hayek of 1944 would approve.

In the last conversation I had with Michael Beesley, I mentioned that I was giving this lecture and he immediately said, 'You must say something new'. His suggestion was to question the regulator's proposal to modify the periodic review process.[22] 'A continuous review would play into the hands of the companies', said Michael. 'How could the regulator possibly cope with such a continual assault? His only hope is to restrict the action to periodic encounters, when he is able to compare all the companies

---

21 Quoted in 'No Minister?' *Fair Trading*, Issue 24, October 1999 pp. 6–8.

22 *Reviews of Public Utility Suppliers 1998 to 2000: Distribution Price Control Review*, Consultation Paper, May 1999, paras 2.10 and 2.11.

simultaneously'. I admit to sympathy with this view. But we need to see any proposals before coming to judgement.

I am pleased that the regulator is taking forward reform of the trading arrangements so as to replace the Pool by more flexible bilateral contracting processes. It is a further example of the need for a regulator to get actively involved in promoting change towards a more competitive market. The proposal has come under fire from numerous consultants, both here and in the US. There may be scope for more precise and sharper locational signals than hitherto proposed, if political constraints allow this. But the fundamental aim, to replace half a market by a two-sided one, and to replace a mechanical price-setting mechanism by prices negotiated in the market process, seems to me a sound one. Whether or not it will also deliver the magnitude of immediate price reductions that some have associated with it, it will reduce the scope for collusion, bring greater flexibility and efficiency, and hence be conducive to lower prices over the longer term.

I am also impressed by the sensitive and constructive way the regulator has handled the government's request for a social action plan to protect disadvantaged customers. He has rightly focused on making the market work more effectively for them, rather than on holding down prices or introducing subsidies.

My final comment concerns the regulator's proposed revision to the supply price restraints.[23] The proposed removal of restraints on non-domestic prices is a further welcome move to an unrestricted market. The maintenance of domestic price restraints is also understandable, at least for a further year, since competition is only just developing. However, it is not so clear why these restraints have to be tightened, or tightened so much, if there are active competitors out there to offer lower prices to customers as a result of predicted lower costs. Is that consistent with protecting the interests of consumers, wherever possible and appropriate by the promotion of effective competition? I do hope that reducing the attractiveness of this market does not drive away existing competitors, discourage new entrants and new services,

---

[23] *Reviews of Public Electricity Suppliers 1998 to 2000: Supply Price Control Review, Initial Proposals*, Ofgem October 1999.

and reinforce the perceived dependence of customers, their representatives and politicians on maximum price regulation in a prospectively competitive sector of this industry.[24]

The pressure on a sector regulator to respond to the concerns expressed by interested parties in that sector, including customers, can be quite significant. The balance of advantage probably lies with the sector regulator when it comes to the detailed knowledge of monopoly regulation, and in pushing through reforms of market structure and operation. There may be merit in transferring regulatory activities in increasingly competitive markets to the Director General of Fair Trading, who has a broader constituency of interests to consider and a broader perspective of competitive markets against which to form judgements on regulatory policy.

7. Conclusions

I have concentrated on the electricity industry because that is the sector I know best. But I suspect that the results and conclusions would be true to a greater or lesser extent for the other utilities that have been privatised, at least in the telecommunications, gas and water industries. In sum, public monopolies have been transformed into regulated private industries exhibiting significant amounts of competition, efficiency improvement, innovation, lower prices (prospectively, in the case of water) and improved quality of service.

I have also limited myself to the UK, although an increasing number of other countries are privatising their utilities, and introducing competition and regulation. In doing so they are reflecting lessons learned from the UK. In electricity, for example, they are typically separating out transmission, creating a Pool, using RPI–X price regulation and allowing competition in supply, as we did. They are often going further in splitting up the generation sector. On the other hand, in my view there is not yet a

---

[24] I later expanded this argument in a short article 'A competitive shock to the system', *Financial Times*, 11 November 1999, p. 21, and a longer paper 'Promoting Competition in Electricity Supply' published on the web-site *www.power-ink.com* and in *Power UK*, No. 68, 29 November 1999, pp. 12–19. The regulator's final proposals (Ofgem, December 1999) went about halfway towards my suggestions.

sufficient appreciation of the need to separate distribution and supply.

From the point of view of market economists, the next steps in the UK are to transfer further, from government to customers, the control and influence over the utility industries. I have suggested reduced government powers and greater regulatory independence from government as means to achieve this. There is also scope to reduce the role of regulation in the increasingly competitive sectors of these industries. A challenge for the future is to develop ways of increasing competition and reducing the role of regulation in the remaining monopoly sectors. But that lies beyond the scope of this paper.

The Wincott Memorial Lectures

1. **The Counter-Revolution in Monetary Theory**
   MILTON FRIEDMAN
   1970 *Occasional Paper 33* 5th Impression 1983 £1.00

2. **Wages and Prices in a Mixed Economy**
   JAMES E. MEADE
   1971 *Occasional Paper 35* Out of print

3. **Government and High Technology**
   JOHN JEWKES
   1972 *Occasional Paper 37* Out of print

4. **Economic Freedom and Representative Government**
   F. A. HAYEK
   1973 *Occasional Paper 39* 3rd Impression 1980
   Out of print

5. **Aspects of Post-war Economic Policy**
   LORD ROBBINS
   1974 *Occasional Paper 42* £1.00

6. **A General Hypothesis of Employment, Inflation and Politics**
   PETER JAY
   1976 *Occasional Paper 46* 2nd Impression 1977 £1.00

7. **The Credibility of Liberal Economics**
   ALAN PEACOCK
   1977 *Occasional Paper 50* Out of print

8. **Economists and the British Economy**
   ALAN WALTERS
   1978 *Occasional Paper 54* £1.00

9. **Choice in European Monetary Union**
   ROLAND VAUBEL
   1979 *Occasional Paper 55* £1.00